REJOICE

and

BE GLAD

GROUP READING GUIDE

to POPE FRANCIS' *Gaudete et Exsultate*

BILL HUEBSCH

**TWENTY-THIRD
PUBLICATIONS**
twentythirdpublications.com

TWENTY-THIRD PUBLICATIONS
One Montauk Avenue, Suite 200, New London, CT 06320
(860) 437-3012 • (800) 321-0411 • www.twentythirdpublications.com

Cover photo: © Stefano Spaziani

ISBN: 978-1-62785-377-4
Printed in the U.S.A.

 A division of Bayard, Inc.

HOW TO USE THIS STUDY GUIDE

Gather. This Reading Guide is designed to be used either alone or with others. If you are sharing in a group, begin by welcoming everyone. Offer a special welcome to participants from other faith traditions who may join you. Ask participants to introduce themselves if needed. As your private or group session gets underway, always begin with the Sign of the Cross.

Divide this document into enough material to fill the time allotted for each of your study or prayer times, or for the amount of time your small group meets. Simply mark your stopping point for each session and take up next time where you left off. Work through the material as quickly or as slowly as you wish.

Read. If you are meeting in a small group, move around the circle and read aloud the stanzas of this summary. Rotate readers with each numbered article. Group members should note items in the pope's teaching that strike them as especially important. (Do not read aloud the article numbers. They are included to help you find each article in the original document if you want to explore in more depth certain elements of this exhortation.)

    If you are using this material for private study, read the material slowly and reflectively.

Discuss and Pray. When you come to the group process notes, pause to continue around the circle, discussing or praying as the notes direct. If you're in private study, put down the booklet and pause at these points to allow the Lord to speak in your meditation; enter into prayerful conversation with him. Group users may do the same between group meetings. Use our discussion and meditation suggestions as a starting point and add your questions, prayers, or action plans.

Finish. As you come to the end of your process in each session, invite participants to identify the one or two large ideas that they hear the Holy Father teaching in that segment of the document. Each participant may hear the text differently; there are no "correct" answers.

Conclude your session with a brief prayer and hospitality.

GAUDETE
et EXSULTATE:
Rejoice and Be Glad

1 Jesus calls us to holiness and asks us for the world! In return, he offers us happiness and clarity about the purpose for which God created us. Jesus calls us to be saints and, from the earliest texts of Scripture, asks us to walk with him, trust in him, and live a holy life.

2 My goal in this reflection is to help everyone hear the call to holiness in his or her particular situation in life. I propose a practical pathway that takes into account "the risks, challenges, and opportunities" that lie before us.

CHAPTER ONE
The Call to Holiness

THE SAINTS WHO ENCOURAGE AND ACCOMPANY US

3 We learn in the Letter to the Hebrews to gather up courage, stamina, and hope, and to "run the race that is set before us." The text assures us that we are not alone but are part of a great crowd of others who help us advance toward the goal of holiness, and these may include our mothers or grandmothers, friends or neighbors, even when their lives were not perfect.

4 For this reason, we can each say that we are guided by "the friends of God." Being in the family of God makes it possible for us to achieve what we could never do alone. The saints who walk with us also protect and guide us; they sustain and carry us when times are difficult.

5 Whenever we canonize a saint, we recognize someone who lived his or her life for others, even up to death. An example for us in this regard is Blessed Maria Gabriella Sagheddu who dedicated her life as a Trappist nun to praying for Christian unity.

THE SAINTS "NEXT DOOR"

6 We aren't thinking here only of those who are already canonized, but also of many others among the People of God. We do not go to the heart of the Lord alone;

we go there only as part of a rich community, blessed by God, called by God, and strengthened by God. God, in other words, draws us to himself as a people in our particular moment in history and place in life.

7 Who are you? Did you ever think God might call you to holiness? Parents who raise your kids with love, you are called. Men and women who work every day to support your families, you are called. Sick and older adults, you are called. Senior members of religious communities, you are called. I like to call this "the middle class of holiness," saints among us who strive to hear God and follow God's way.

8 Yes, the humblest members of our community are often the ones whom God chooses to be a model for us all. As Vatican II taught in chapter twelve of the great *Constitution on the Church*, all the baptized share in the prophetic work of witnessing to God's love. They touch our lives in ways we don't always see or understand. Saint Teresa Benedicta of the Cross reminds us that we may not know until we are in the light of heaven about all those whose loving touch formed and shaped us.

9 All Christians experience this call to holiness, and people also experience it beyond the Christian faith as God works in his mysterious ways. Holiness is "the most attractive face of the Church" because when men and women sacrifice themselves on behalf of others, it is compelling.

FOR GROUP PROCESS OR PERSONAL REFLECTION

Holiness, the Holy Father teaches, is lived in everyday life when we open our hearts to grace and practice self-giving love in our normal, daily routine. What are some examples from your own life when you have seen this in others or yourself?

Who are "the saints next door" in your experience?

THE LORD CALLS

10 I want to focus here primarily on the call to holiness that the Lord has sounded in each of our hearts. Again, as the *Constitution on the Church* teaches in article eleven, the Lord calls all the faithful, regardless their state in life, to holiness. This call isn't reserved only for the ordained or religious. God calls each of us by name.

11 We should not become discouraged or begin to think that we are not worthy or capable of holiness. If we know about someone who has given himself or herself completely, such as St. Teresa of Calcutta, we should not think that we can never do what she did. We are not meant to copy St. Teresa or anyone else; God has called her to that mission, but that doesn't mean God has called us to the same work. God calls each of us to our own mission, and we must follow "the specific path the Lord has in mind for us." There are many ways to be holy witnesses to God's love, as St. John of the Cross has reminded us.

12 There have been, for example, many holy women such as Saints Hildegard, Bridget, Catherine of Siena, Teresa of Ávila, or Thérèse of Lisieux. But there have also been many forgotten women whose courage and faith helped transform the family or society in which they lived.

13 I hope this will excite us! I hope it will encourage us to discern how the Lord is calling each of us. As God taught us in Jeremiah (1:5), "Before I formed you in the womb, I knew you, and before you were born, I consecrated you."

FOR YOU, TOO

14 Again, to be holy doesn't mean we must be ordained or join a religious order. We're tempted to believe that holiness means withdrawing from everyday life. In fact, being holy means living our lives with love and giving witness to that in everything we do. If you're called to be a religious sister, then do that with joy and commitment. If you're called to be married, love and care for your spouse. If you're called to work for a living, do so with integrity. If you're called to be a grandparent, teach the little ones to love Jesus. If you're called to be in authority, work for the common good.

15 Be open to God in whatever situation you find yourself in life. Remember, you have the power of the Spirit within you who gives you all the strength and courage you need for this. Also, you have the Church and, in the Church, you have the guiding hand of God through Scripture, liturgy, holy places, and a whole crowd of saints.

16 The kind of holiness I'm describing here is lived in small ways most of the time. For example, a woman goes shopping and meets a neighbor; she avoids gossip. Later, her children need her time; she gives it even if she is tired. She feels anxiety, so she prays. Later, she meets a homeless person, but she stops to say a kind word to him or her. Each moment is a step toward holiness.

17 We live this holiness in the particular situation in which we find ourselves each day.

18 We can live with this kind of everyday holiness because God gives us the grace to do it. Grace empowers us, it fills us with God's own life, and it is always enough for whatever we are called to do. No matter what weakness or life situation we are in, grace is powerful enough to help us live with love.

FOR GROUP PROCESS OR PERSONAL REFLECTION

*As the Holy Father teaches in article 11,
we are each called to holiness in the concrete and specific
circumstances of our life. We live that holiness in many small ways
every day. Think back over the past week as you reread
article 16. What are the many small occasions for a
holy response to people or situations that you
have experienced in your life?*

YOUR MISSION IN CHRIST

19 God gives each of us a mission in life, and we live that out in our specific moment of time.

20 The fullest meaning of our lifelong mission is to reflect the self-giving love of Jesus, to die to ourselves in every aspect of our life. In doing this, we echo the earthly life of Christ himself: our private times and our communal times, our encounters with outcasts and the poor, and all the ways in which he showed his self-giving love. As we meditate on Christ's life, we gradually incorporate his ministry into our own lives.

21 God is love, and holiness is living in that divine love and charity based on the example of Jesus. Each of our lives is a message to the world, and the message is the same: God loves you; he walks with you; he has given himself entirely for you, and now he calls you to do the same.

22 The Lord speaks through your life, but let's not get caught up in the small things you may do. You will make mistakes and experience failure; not everything a saint says or does is holy. But don't give up because it is the totality of your life that matters.

23 I invite you to listen closely to God in prayer and recognize how your call to holiness is embedded in the people, activities, and situations of your daily life. I invite you to "allow the Spirit to forge in you" how you will show the face of God to the world.

24 May you come to know the message that God wants to speak to the world through your life. May you let yourself be renewed and filled with the Holy Spirit. You're on a mission, as I said above, one that is unique to you. Even if you make mistakes and fail, God stays with you and holds you up; God gives you strength and remains with you. You have all the grace needed for your mission.

FOR GROUP PROCESS OR PERSONAL REFLECTION

*What messages is God speaking to the world
through your life? How is that message communicated
through your activities and words?*

*Pause to enter into conversation with the Lord,
listen to his voice as he calls and loves you.
If appropriate, share your prayer experience with others.*

ACTIVITY THAT SANCTIFIES

25 Remember that the call to holiness we're exploring here is also and at the same time a call to build the Reign of God. The two are inseparable. You will experience great happiness in your life when you learn the art of self-giving love and give yourself to this mission, body and soul.

26 In a sense, we're each called to become a "contemplative" in the midst of a busy life of service and love. Being a contemplative doesn't mean withdrawing to a quiet place and never coming back. It means, rather, loving silence while interacting with others; finding peace and quiet while working hard for justice; seeking prayer while serving your family, community, or the Church.

27 Engagement with the world is not "second best" to prayer and contemplation. They go hand-in-hand. The pathway to interior peace and holiness is the same as the pathway to building up the Reign of God. It isn't so much that we have accepted an arbitrary call to mission as that our very lives, oriented to God and flowing from the Spirit, *are* a mission.

28 If our very being in the world is the mission on which God has sent us, then we must embrace that with humility and peace of heart. The "spirituality of your life" connects you to your family, work, and society.

29 This does not mean we should avoid quiet and contemplation. Quite the contrary! Noisy gadgets and distractions fill today's world. If we are going to hear God's voice in this din, then we must step back and be in dialogue with the Lord. In the midst of all our daily work, we can find time for this. So, when a quiet moment presents itself, when we awaken in the night, as we prepare to pray the Mass—these are times when this dialogue may occur. And when we are in crisis, all the more do we find it necessary to speak with the Lord.

30 We must guard against the temptation to be buried in modern technology or busyness because this can draw us away from our mission and from being our truest self.

31 I invite you to develop a spirit of holiness, one that will be evident in both your solitude and your service. In this way, every moment of your life can be an expression of self-giving love and a step along the pathway to holiness.

FOR GROUP PROCESS OR PERSONAL REFLECTION
How do you balance prayer with activity?
How much time do you spend with technology each day?
How much time in prayer and contemplation?
How much time doing your daily work?

CHAPTER TWO

Two Subtle Enemies of Holiness

35 I would like to discuss now two false forms of holiness. They're both heresies from the early years of the Church, but they've never gone away completely. We call one by the name Gnosticism or intellectualism, whereby people are judged worthy (or not worthy) based on their intellectual grasp of certain doctrines, whether or not their hearts are in Christ. We call the other by the name Pelagianism or individualism, whereby people believe that by the power of their individual will rather than by the grace of Christ they can attain goodness and salvation.

Rather than opening the door to grace in a person's life, these errors tend to close that down. On the one hand, Gnostics believe that only a grasp of doctrine determines whether or not we are faithful. On the other, Pelagians believe we are saved by our own efforts and initiative. Neither leaves much room for Christ, grace, mystery, or our neighbor.

CONTEMPORARY GNOSTICISM

36 Gnosticism is concerned with a set of theories or ideas, with *knowing about* God but not necessarily *walking with* God and experiencing God's love.

An intellect without God and without flesh

37 Thank goodness the Church has long taught that God measures people by the charity in their hearts rather than by the knowledge they possess. Gnostics or intellectuals judge others based on how well they understand Church teaching. To them, the intellect is separate from the body somehow, as though they exist in a dual universe. But of course, Christ is in the flesh as much today as ever, and so are we all. That God is in the flesh is the mystery of the Incarnation. We cannot separate the mystery of our faith from the body of Christ.

38 People are attracted to this intellectual approach because it appears to be so pure and orderly. Everything appears to fit into a tidy ecclesial system, but what's missing is the real suffering of the people whom Christ loves.

39 Gnostics or intellectuals believe that their explanations can somehow make everything in the mystery of Christ and God fully understandable. We applaud the use of reason to reflect on theology; that's a good thing. But to reduce the marvels of Jesus and his message to a "cold and harsh logic" is going too far.

A doctrine without mystery

40 One of the most sinister aspects of Gnosticism or intellectualism is that it considers its tidy system of doctrine and dogma to be perfect. But by taming mystery in this way and attempting to corner the market on grace, it ignores the mystery of God's grace as it is demonstrated in people's lives.

41 We must always remember that God is God. God is a divine mystery and transcends our human minds and intellects. "When somebody has an answer for every question, it is a sign that they are not on the right road." God is acting in our lives, and often we don't know it until we look back over our shoulder to see the hand of God. We don't know precisely when or how we will encounter Christ. The exact time or place of this encounter remains a mystery and is not up to us. So, people who believe they know everything about God, as I said, are presuming to control how God acts in people's lives.

42 Who knows how God might be present in someone else's life? Even if a person appears to be living in a disastrous state, with public vices or sins, God is still present. The Spirit can help us see God's presence in every situation, but Gnostic thinking won't allow for this because it cannot control it.

FOR GROUP PROCESS OR PERSONAL REFLECTION

What is your experience of Gnosticism or intellectualism in the Church? In your life?

How does the mystery of God unfold in your life?
In the lives of people you know and love?
What is your response to article 41?

The limits of reason

43 Coming to understand what the Lord has taught us is difficult enough, and expressing it in modern language is even more difficult. There are legitimately different ways to express many aspects of doctrine, and they all add to the richness of God's word. I know that those who prefer a uniform, rigid system of formulas for doctrine find this undesirable, but regional and personal differences are our legacy and long history.

44 How we express doctrine is not a closed system. People's questions, their struggles, their failures, their dreams and worries—all contribute to how the Church makes doctrine and belief part of our real, everyday lives.

45 In certain Gnostic circles, people might even think that they are saints already simply because they can articulate doctrine so perfectly, not like the "ignorant masses" who struggle to believe. But God's love is offered to all; like a seamless garment, there are no more noble or less noble people in the sight of God.

46 St. Francis of Assisi can help us here. He noted that St. Anthony of Padua was teaching the brothers theology. He counseled Anthony to be careful that the theology was never separated from the spirit of prayer and devotion, that it was never "disembodied." Francis knew that we cannot reduce the Christian life to a few intellectual formulas, but that it had to remain close to the freshness—and mystery—of the gospel. St. Bonaventure taught that any intellectual exercise must lead to mercy. Works of mercy and prayer, he taught, are the building blocks of intellectual wisdom.

FOR GROUP PROCESS OR PERSONAL REFLECTION
In your own words, what is Gnosticism or
intellectualism as the Holy Father describes it here?
Why is it a danger to the faith?

CONTEMPORARY PELAGIANISM

47 Over time, Gnosticism was replaced by another error. People realized that it isn't knowledge that makes us holy, but it is the life we lead. The focus on how we live led to a second error that we still have with us today, Pelagianism.

48 In the same way that Gnostics attributed power to the intellect, people began to attribute power to people's personal efforts to be good. Rather than replacing grace and mystery with intelligence, these latter ones replaced it with the human will. Who needs God if by our own wills we can save ourselves? But as Paul wrote to the Romans (9:16) everything we need for salvation "depends not on human will or exertion, but on God who shows mercy." And remember what we learned in the First Letter of John (4:19): We can love because "he first loved us." The initiative is always on God's part.

A will lacking humility

49 There are those in the Church who speak about God's grace with confidence and assurance, but in the end, they trust only in their own powers. These often feel superior to those whom they deem to be weaker than they are. They feel superior because they obey certain rules or remain stubbornly attached to a certain Catholic style. They criticize and counsel others, saying that Christ can accomplish all things in us, but deep down, they mean that others should overcome their "weaknesses" and, by their own will, follow the teachings more closely. These forget that, as Bonaventure taught, not everyone can measure up this way. Or, as Augustine taught, God wants us to do what we can and ask for what we cannot do.

50 In the end, we must acknowledge our weaknesses before God. Only then will God's grace seize us and work within us. Grace builds on nature gradually; it doesn't make us into superhumans overnight. Learning to trust God's grace is a process of admitting our sins and realizing that, despite them—and their number is legion— God holds nothing against us, and he chooses us. We live with concrete, specific limitations, all of us do, but grace operates within that. Slowly, grace moves us ever more toward the heart of God. If we come to believe somehow that we move along this pathway on our own, we block the very grace we need.

51 We have often said in spiritual circles that "God dwells in us," but it would be better to say that "we dwell in God." God invites us to walk with him and trust him. God has given us life and love. Once we accept that this comes from God and not from our own will, we are on the pathway.

FOR GROUP PROCESS OR PERSONAL REFLECTION

The Holy Father here is teaching that we all live with human weakness and limitations. Very few of us attain perfection! Why is it necessary for us to depend on grace rather than our own will for healing? What is your response to article 50?

An overlooked Church teaching

52 The Church has continually taught that only the grace of the Lord draws us closer to the divine heart. The initiative, as I said above, always comes from God. St. John Chrysostom wrote that God gives us the gifts we need. St. Basil taught we glory in God alone because we know we lack what we need.

53 Since the Second Synod of Orange in 529, we have taught that we cannot earn grace, cannot purchase it, and do not deserve it. It taught that even the desire to cooperate with grace comes to us as grace. The Council of Trent affirmed this.

54 The *Catechism of the Catholic Church* likewise reminds us that grace is a gift, pure and simple. God's unbelievable love for us, God's generous forgiveness of our sins, the power God gives us to do good and avoid what is evil—these are all gifts. We simply receive them with joy.

55 This great belief of the Church is ancient. We hold firmly to it. We have continually taught this because it is rooted in Scripture. Let us accept it with happiness and admit that our whole life is a gift.

56 It is true that we cooperate with grace and must take the initiative to do that, but first and foremost, we belong to God. We have always taught that charity is what "makes growth in the life of grace possible." Indeed, as we read in the First Letter to the Corinthians (13:2), "If I do not have love, I am nothing."

New Pelagians

57 Even though all this is true and has long been our teaching, some Christians believe that their own efforts and abilities are what bring them to God. Some might have an obsession with law and order in the Church. These believe that the rules can save us. Or they might be utterly absorbed in social or political advantage, believing that they are saved by their privilege. Or they might be scrupulous about liturgical details, believing that just getting it right will save us. Or they may be focused on the administration of the Church or excessively committed to self-help programs of various kinds. Rather than passion and excitement for how the Spirit leads people to love, or rather than outreach to people who thirst for Christ, these people focus attention on minor facets of the Church.

58 The attitude that only rubrics and rules matter often leads to a church that is a museum piece. Or it may lead to a church that belongs only to a select few who give excessive attention to rules, customs, or ways of doing liturgy. These attitudes reduce and constrict the gospel.

59 When this happens, we obscure the gospel and make it complicated for people. Rather than being the "good news," it becomes a burden.

The summation of the Law

60 To avoid this neo-Pelagian way of thinking, we should remember that there is a hierarchy of values and virtues in the Scriptures. The central virtue is charity. The whole law is summed up in this one virtue, as Galatians tells us (5:14): "You shall love your neighbor as yourself." It's no more complicated than that.

61 Jesus cleans out this forest of Pelagian and Gnostic thinking. He asks us simply to see two faces. One is the face of Abba, and the other the face of our sister or brother. These aren't rules or commands but faces. Or perhaps it is one face, that of the Father reflected for us in others. We find God, not in rubrics or excessive doctrine, but in the face of the most vulnerable, the most defenseless, those most in need of our mercy.

62 May the Lord set us free from both Gnosticism and Pelagianism. They weigh down the message of Christ and block people along the pathway to holiness. I invite you personally to reflect and discern before God whether either of these might be present in your life.

FOR GROUP PROCESS OR PERSONAL REFLECTION

The Holy Father is pointing out in article 57 that Pelagianism or the idea that we can be saved without grace may take many forms. In your own words, how do you see this playing out in your life or the Church? What other forms of Pelagianism do you see?

CHAPTER THREE

In the Light of the Master

63 There are many ways to describe holiness, but none of them is more compelling than turning to Jesus' own words. What did he teach us? With characteristic simplicity, Jesus taught us the Beatitudes, and they have become our identity and calling card as Christians. When someone asks, "How do I become holy?" the Beatitudes answer. Follow them in your daily life.

64 In them, first and foremost, we learn that being blessed or happy is the same as being holy. Self-giving love leads to true and deep joy.

GOING AGAINST THE FLOW

65 The words of Jesus are poetic in the Sermon on the Mount where the Beatitudes are found, but they're also profound. "The world pushes us towards another way of living." When we are living in the Holy Spirit, however, we have the power to be freed from weakness and made strong in Christ.

66 Let's reflect now on Jesus' words. Let them challenge us anew. Let them "demand a real change in the way we live."

Blessed are the poor in spirit, for theirs is the kingdom of heaven

67 When we look into the depths of our heart, where do we find security in life? Is it about money and wealth? Jesus teaches that these are fleeting; he speaks of the rich fool (Luke 12:16–21), the one who felt secure because he was financially set. Rich, yes, but he didn't realize that he could die on that very day and then what good would his wealth have done him?

68 Wealth is false security. It often squeezes out God's word, the care of those around us, or the ability to enjoy life. Wealth can cause us to miss the greatest treasure of all, which is to allow Christ into our hearts.

69 St. Ignatius calls us to another way of life, "holy indifference." Holy indifference leads us to keep the work of the Lord before all the small elements of life—and in doing so, we experience real freedom. For example, suppose you have a closet full of shoes and clothing that you treasure greatly. On your way to the store one day, you meet a homeless man shivering in the cold. At this point, holiness calls you to be indifferent toward your clothing, so you meet the man, give him your sweater, and begin to follow the teaching of the Lord to love your neighbor. We can't love our clothing more than "the least of my brothers and sisters" (Matthew 25). We learn to say, "I like all my clothing and shoes, but loving my neighbor is much more important."

70 Likewise, Luke speaks, not of the poor in spirit but of the materially poor. He invites us to live a plain life, not bound up in wealth, so that we can share with those most in need. In this way, we become like Jesus who "made himself poor" (2 Corinthians 8:9). Being poor of heart leads to holiness.

FOR GROUP PROCESS OR PERSONAL REFLECTION

What strikes you in how the Holy Father presents this Beatitude? What challenges you? How does this teaching of the Lord lead to blessed happiness?

Blessed are the meek, for they will inherit the earth

71 The world is filled with conflict. Everyone thinks that their own political, cultural, or social views and customs are correct, even about how people dress or speak. In the midst of this, Jesus proposes a way of thinking that seems impossible: be meek, he teaches. We see him practicing this with his disciples.

72 "Learn from me," Christ teaches us, "for I am gentle and humble of heart" (Matthew 11:29). We become weary when we are constantly upset with how others live and when we spend our energy judging and comparing. But Jesus teaches us to take a meek attitude, one of patience and tenderness with others, without any air of superiority toward them.

73 Paul urges us to be cautious about correcting others, to be meek when doing so, because we may find the same fault within ourselves (Galatians 6:1). Even if we are defending our faith, we should do so with meekness (1 Peter 3:16), and that includes how we treat our enemies (2 Timothy 2:25). "In the Church, we have often erred by not embracing this demand of God's word."

74 Meekness leads us to interior poverty. It renders us ready to trust in God, to step back from confrontation long enough to put our hope in the Lord. We replace fear, anger, and aggression with fullness of heart and peace. Reacting with meekness and humility is what leads to holiness.

FOR GROUP PROCESS OR PERSONAL REFLECTION

*What strikes you in how the Holy Father presents
this Beatitude? What challenges you? How does this
teaching of the Lord lead to blessed happiness?*

Blessed are those who mourn, for they will be comforted

75 In our modern times, we shun and avoid sickness and sorrow. We try to fill up our thoughts with pleasures and escapes. We think that this leads to "the good life." We spend of a lot of energy avoiding suffering, but we can never avoid the cross. It is always present.

76 Pain and sorrow are real. When we share in the suffering of others, we help reduce it. Knowing that we give comfort and aid in the name of Jesus helps us to be uninhibited about reaching out and drawing others near to us. The feeling of compassion replaces our discomfort, and we become healers. Knowing how to mourn with others leads to happiness.

FOR GROUP PROCESS OR PERSONAL REFLECTION

*What strikes you in how the Holy Father presents
this Beatitude? What challenges you? How does this
teaching of the Lord lead to blessed happiness?*

Blessed are those who hunger and thirst for righteousness, for they will be filled

77 Being hungry or thirsty is a powerful feeling. Having hunger and thirst for justice is likewise a powerful force.

78 It's easy for us to see injustice but become complacent toward it. Petty personal interests and the temptation to greed and corruption fill the world. The poor stand and watch while the rich "divvy up the good things of this life." Inequality is so pervasive that it is easy for us to give up the fight for justice.

79 True justice occurs when we make decisions about money and business that are just. Our decisions about the care of the poor and vulnerable are especially important because they are so close to the heart of Jesus. Hungering for justice is a key building block of holiness.

Blessed are the merciful, for they will receive mercy

80 Mercy has two faces. The first face is that of helping others and having mercy on those most in need. The second is that of forgiveness and kind understanding of people's situations. Do unto others, Matthew teaches in his gospel, as you would have them do unto you (7:12).

81 Mercy involves both giving and forgiving. When we do this, we reflect God's actions toward us. God has given us everything and forgiven us endlessly. Luke teaches us to "be merciful, even as your Father is merciful" (6:36). We are merciful, in other words, because God has shown us so much mercy. Luke goes a bit further, however, and we should remember this: "The measure you give will be the measure you get back" (6:38).

82 Recall the parable of the unmerciful servant in Matthew. The man had been himself forgiven by his master, but then went out and withheld mercy from a fellow slave, demanding payment. "We need to think of ourselves as an army of the forgiven." In whose name would we withhold mercy from someone else? Certainly not in God's name! Acting with mercy creates holiness within us.

Blessed are the pure in heart, for they will see God

83 God wants to give us a new heart (Ezekiel 36:26). The new heart will be one that is burning with the desire to love.

84 God knows what is in our hearts. He knows when we are false or insincere.

85 It is certainly true that we must undertake works of love, but they must flow from a pure heart, one motivated by love. Recall what we learn in the First Letter to the Corinthians, "If I give away all I have … but have not love, I gain nothing" (13:3). The intentions of our heart are what defile us. Even when our actions appear to be generous, if our hearts are treacherous, we gain nothing.

86 The gospel invites us to give our heart to God and our neighbor and to be genuine in doing so. Giving away our heart is how we see God, for God is love. Keeping our heart free from false love and deep in God's love leads to holiness.

> **FOR GROUP PROCESS OR PERSONAL REFLECTION**
> *What strikes you in how the Holy Father presents*
> *this Beatitude? What challenges you? How does this*
> *teaching of the Lord lead to blessed happiness?*

Blessed are the peacemakers, for they will be called children of God

87 The world rages with war. But even in our daily lives, we can cause pain and misunderstanding. Spreading gossip, even if it is true, causes such harm. Those who gossip are the enemies of peace.

88 Peacemakers do just what the word implies, they "make peace happen" by working for it. The writers of the New Testament constantly urge the Christian community to "pursue what makes for peace" (Romans 14:19).

89 Making peace is not easy. We want to include everyone, even those who seem "a bit odd, troublesome or difficult, demanding, different, beaten down by life or simply uninterested." Our hearts and minds must be open to the ideas of others. And in peacemaking, we cannot ignore conflict but face it and resolve it. Sowing peace is the pathway to holiness.

FOR GROUP PROCESS OR PERSONAL REFLECTION

*What strikes you in how the Holy Father presents
this Beatitude? What challenges you? How does this
teaching of the Lord lead to blessed happiness?*

*Blessed are those who are persecuted for righteousness' sake,
for theirs is the kingdom of heaven*

90 Make no mistake about this: Jesus warns us that this long road to holiness, with its many facets and elements, will go against the flow of society. We may find ourselves challenging the status quo, and doing that is never comfortable. But this is our calling. "Unless we wish to sink into an obscure mediocrity, let us not long for an easy life."

91 We know that living according to the gospel will not be easy. Society and its organization surrounding production and consumption, the place of the poor, and the entanglement of all this with the churches—these are one of the obstacles we must face. Again, living the Beatitudes will not be easy; people will view us negatively. They will be suspicious of us. We will meet with ridicule.

92 We cling to the cross at these times. Persecution is part of the equation of the Paschal Mystery.

93 The persecution we will face will not be from everyone. Indeed, Acts of the Apostles tells us that the early Church enjoyed the favor of the local people (2:47). But those in authority did not want to hear this truth.

94 The persecution we face today may include the shedding of our blood, and we have plenty of examples of modern martyrs. But it will also include more subtle means, such as slander, lies, undermining, and times when people will "utter all kinds of evil against you falsely on my account" (Matthew 5:11). But accepting the daily pathway of gospel living leads to holiness, so brace yourselves.

FOR GROUP PROCESS OR PERSONAL REFLECTION

What strikes you in how the Holy Father presents this Beatitude? What challenges you? How does this teaching of the Lord lead to blessed happiness?

THE GREAT CRITERION

95 Jesus gives us one clear criterion on which God will ultimately judge us as holy or not. We find it in the twenty-fifth chapter of Matthew, and it elaborates on the Beatitude in which he taught that the merciful would be blessed.

In fidelity to the Master

96 "Holiness, then, is not about swooning in mystic rapture." If we would be holy, we must learn to see Jesus in the faces of those whom he most loved: the poor. The text in Matthew 25:35–36 is much more than a mere invitation to do good or to be charitable. This text helps us understand the mystery of Christ. It teaches us that when we see the poor, we also see Christ. We experience his heart and his own deepest priorities and choices. It's that simple.

97 Because the gospel is so clear, it is my duty as pope to invite all Christians to embrace Christ in the poor, without any ifs, ands, or buts. The Lord himself made it clear that holiness cannot be separated from the demand as stated in Matthew 25: Whatever you do to the least of my sisters or brothers, you do to me.

98 For example, when we encounter a homeless person on a cold night, we have some choices. We can see the homeless as a bother, an ugly blemish on our city, a lazy person, a problem for someone else to fix, or even just a piece of litter on a busy street. Or I can look into his or her face and see Christ. I can see a fellow human being with as much dignity as I have, and someone whom God loves as much as God loves me. "Can holiness somehow be understood apart from this lively recognition of the dignity of each human being?" The answer is "no."

99 This makes us uneasy and uncomfortable, and it should. For us Christians, this means we must seek social change that will restore justice for all.

FOR GROUP PROCESS OR PERSONAL REFLECTION
What strikes you in how the Holy Father presents
this teaching from Matthew 25? What challenges you?
How does this teaching of the Lord shape and frame
your life? How do you respond to article 98?

Ideologies striking at the heart of the Gospel

100 I wish to point out two errors in thinking that sometimes arise. First, there is the error of those Christians who somehow separate the demands of the gospel from their everyday faith, from their relationship with the Lord and his grace. We cannot do this! Saints Francis of Assisi, Vincent de Paul, and Teresa of Calcutta help us see that there is a strong connection between prayer, our love of God, and our commitment to those most in need of mercy.

101 The second error is found in those who believe that the social engagement of others is somehow not spiritual, that it is worldly and secular. These believe that there are more important matters than the care of the poor and that the only thing that matters is the one issue that they defend. An example of this is our defense of the unborn. Certainly, we must be clear, firm, and passionate about caring for the unborn since life is at stake. But equally important are the born! We must care for the poor, the abandoned, those who are underprivileged, infirm, elderly, or victims of slavery and human trafficking, and all other forms of rejection. Doing so does not detract from our defense of life but is part and parcel of it. It is especially true that we cannot turn a blind eye to the distribution of wealth in today's world. We cannot offer moral support for a system in which rich people lavish goods and comfort on themselves while the poor look on from abject poverty.

FOR GROUP PROCESS OR PERSONAL REFLECTION

*What strikes you in how the Holy Father presents
this teaching about the born and the unborn?
What challenges you?*

*Read the last two sentences of article 101 again.
Where do you fall on the spectrum between wealth and
comfort versus poverty and daily discomfort?*

102 A stunning example of this is our attitude toward migrants. Some Catholics consider the plight of migrants to be a lesser issue, behind what they consider graver issues, especially bioethical questions. No Christian can believe that! Can we not hear the voice of Jesus teaching us that when we welcome the stranger, we welcome him? (Matthew 25:35). St. Benedict ordered that his monks should welcome any guest who knocked on the monastery door as though they were welcoming Christ himself, even if it made the life of the monks a bit more complicated.

103 The Old Testament teaches the same. "The stranger who resides with you shall be to you as the citizen among you, and you shall love him as yourself," the text tells us in Leviticus 19. Welcoming the migrant and the stranger isn't some modern fad or something dreamed up by the pope. God has always taught his people to welcome warmly those who need our assistance. Think of the parable of the good Samaritan in the gospel. Caring for those in need isn't new to us, but it is a teaching that I think we prefer to ignore or forget.

> **FOR GROUP PROCESS OR PERSONAL REFLECTION**
> *In our society today, how does this ancient teaching about welcoming strangers and migrants play out? What is the Christian response?*
>
> *Is there ever a time when we should turn people away from our nation or community? In whose name would we turn them away?*

The worship most acceptable to God

104 We do not give glory to God only when we pray and worship, or by following certain ethical norms. The true and final criterion on which God will judge us, as we just read in Matthew 25, is how we have treated others. Our worship, in fact, becomes pleasing to God only when it leads us to serve.

105 Prayer must transform us into people of mercy. Prayer cannot lead us to any other point because mercy is the foundation of the Church's very life. And the mercy of which we speak always leads to justice and truth.

106 St. Thomas Aquinas was asked which external acts (such as prayer, obedience, or fasting) most effectively show our love for God. Without hesitation, he answered that it is works of mercy toward our neighbor.

107 If you want to grow in holiness and honor God with your life, then be single-minded in the practice of mercy. St. Teresa of Calcutta realized this. "God...depends on us to love the world and to show how much he loves it," she said.

108 When we are preoccupied with all our possessions, homes, and desire for pleasure, we become desperate, and we find it difficult to show mercy to others. But when we cultivate simplicity and resist the feverish demands for consumerism, we become rich. Likewise, when we are caught up in the superficial and unending flow of information in our age, we become deaf to the cry of the poor. But when we tune our ear to those around us, we gain a sense of well-being.

109 The way of Jesus is not complicated, but it is practical and available to everyone. Shaped by the Beatitudes and the criterion of the final judgment in Matthew 25, we become holy. We become saintly. I invite you to read and reread these texts frequently because they will make you genuinely happy.

FOR GROUP PROCESS OR PERSONAL REFLECTION

What is your overall response to this challenging chapter
of the exhortation? Read aloud the Beatitudes in Matthew 5:3–12
and the Great Judgment in Matthew 25:31–46. Afterward, enter
into silent conversation with the Lord about these texts and how
they fit into your life. Share that with others and discuss how
they fit into your society or local community and parish.

CHAPTER FOUR

Signs of Holiness in Today's World

110   We turn now to consider five signs or spiritual attitudes that are necessary for holiness. I will not deal here with certain other obvious holiness practices. We have many methods of prayer. We have the Eucharist and reconciliation, whose value we cannot measure because it is so great. We know about the offering of personal sacrifice, various forms of devotion, spiritual direction, and others.

111   The five signs I will discuss here will not exhaust our treatment of holiness, but they do point the way with clarity and force. They outweigh all the negative forces around us.

PERSEVERANCE, PATIENCE, AND MEEKNESS

112   First, we must be fundamentally oriented toward and grounded in God. It is God's love that sustains us. God's love supports us when there are ups and downs. When you see the peace of the saints, you know they are grounded in this first sign. The inner strength that being oriented toward God provides allows us to be constant in doing good, being faithful, and staying holy for the long term.

113 Being grounded in God helps us "put away all bitterness and wrath..." (Ephesians 4:31).

114 Everyone has aggressive and selfish inclinations, but we must learn to pull them out like weeds and not let them take root. Prayer is our help here. It leads us to peace.

115 We can be caught up in verbal violence through social media, overstep the limits of charity, and hurt others "from a distance." We must keep all the commandments, including the eighth, which forbids both gossip that is true and gossip that is false.

116 Grace leads to meekness of heart. Let us not waste energy complaining about others and their supposed faults. Let's not treat others harshly.

117 Holiness does not lead us to look down on others like "heartless judges." It isn't our job to teach people a lesson when we think they need it. Judging others and trying to correct them is a subtle form of violence. St. John of the Cross taught that we should "always prefer to be taught by all rather than to desire to teach even the least of all." He added that we should be happy to see the good of others and give them precedence over us in all things. Putting others first leads to holiness.

118 Suffering and being humiliated are signs we are on the road to holiness. Suffering comes with the commitment to follow Jesus Christ. He was humiliated in public; he suffered "leaving you an example so that you might follow in his steps" (1 Peter 2:21). Jesus also revealed the humility of God the Father whose love is so tender and so self-effacing that he forgives us time and again when we don't deserve it and even when we don't ask for it.

119 I'm not speaking only about martyrdom. I'm also talking about the daily humiliation that workers suffer to support their families. About people who prefer to praise others rather than boast about themselves. And about those who choose to bear injustice on behalf of others, even endangering their own lives. This meekness doesn't mean keeping your mouth shut. In fact, precisely because we have so little to lose, we speak up to disagree gently, to demand justice, and to defend the weak, even when it harms our reputation.

120 It isn't that such humiliation is fun; it isn't at all! And on a rational level, it's hard to explain. But it is a grace to be requested in prayer: "Lord, when humiliations come, help me to know that I am following in your footsteps."

121 We persevere in our holiness and faith because we know God is with us in all things. Christ becomes our peace, and we know that he came "to guide our feet into the way of peace" (Luke 1:79).

> **FOR GROUP PROCESS OR PERSONAL REFLECTION**
> *In your own words, define the sign of holiness that the*
> *Holy Father is teaching us here. How do you understand these*
> *elements of the spiritual life to fit into your call to holiness?*

JOY AND A SENSE OF HUMOR

122 Holiness leads us to have a sense of humor. Some people think that to be holy is to be always very serious: no smiles or happiness. But the Christian life is one in which there is "joy in the Holy Spirit" (Romans 14:17).

123 Throughout the history of our relationship with God, from the time of the early prophets and psalm writers, happiness in God has been a theme. Faith leads to joy.

124 Mary herself rejoiced. As Jesus did his work among the people, they also rejoiced. The text of the gospel repeatedly reminds us that being in Christ leads to peace and happiness. As Jesus assured us, "You will be sorrowful, but your sorrow will turn into joy" (John 16:20).

125   Why so much joy? Because we are forgiven and loved, endlessly, generously, and eternally. Being loved in this way gives us a deep sense of abiding joy; we know that we walk with Christ.

126   And Christian joy "is usually accompanied by a sense of humor." Yes, humor. Laughter and enjoyment are signs of holiness.

127   As we study the texts of Scripture we learn that God "wants us to be positive, grateful, and uncomplicated." We see everything that is before us as a gift, and our gratitude leads to joy.

128   Christian joy isn't superficial happiness, such as the fleeting sense of pleasure we get from buying things or having them. We experience deep and genuine happiness; such joy leads us to share generously all that we have with others and to do so with cheer.

FOR GROUP PROCESS OR PERSONAL REFLECTION

In your own words, define the sign of holiness that the Holy Father is teaching us here. How do you understand these elements of the spiritual life to fit into your call to holiness?

BOLDNESS AND PASSION

129   Holiness leads us to be bold, to speak up without fear. Jesus is with us, and this gives us courage. We experience tremendous freedom because, despite what the world says, we know that we are living with God.

130   A lack of boldness or passion is a sign that our holiness must grow. Trusting the Lord, we give up our hesitancy; we leave behind the shallow waters near the shore and put out into the deep where we let down our nets.

131 Jesus was not timid, or perhaps he allowed grace to empower him beyond timidity. He actively sought out the sick, preached to the masses, and set people free.

132 Boldness is a sign that the Spirit is with us. It gives us absolute certainty.

133 The apostles experienced this. Locked behind closed doors, filled with fear and afraid to go out, they prayed. What happened next? You know the story: "When they had prayed, the place in which they were gathered together was shaken; and they were all filled with the Holy Spirit and spoke the word of God with boldness" (Acts 4:31).

134 I know there is always a temptation to find safety and security somewhere. We like what is familiar, so we hide behind rules and regulations. We become pessimistic about the world and our mission in it. We dwell in nostalgia and long for the "good old days." We reject new ideas. We live in a world of piety, but we never let it lead us to action.

135 "God is eternal newness." Rather than small and ancient, God is large in his love and modern in his presence. When we let our hearts rest with him, he compels us, leads us, or sometimes maybe drags us out to where our sisters and brothers are most wounded. "God is not afraid!" I invite you to go out to the fringes of society as Jesus did; go there, and you will find people who are wounded, troubled, and desolate—waiting for your healing touch.

136 We often speak of opening the doors of our hearts to Jesus, but I wonder if it isn't the other way around. I think Jesus is already with us, knocking on our door, calling us out of our sanctuaries and chapels to do the work of the Reign of God.

137 We must shun complacency because it is seductive. Complacency lulls us into thinking that nothing will ever change and that things will always be this bad, and that there's nothing we can do, so we might as well give up. Such pessimism isn't the way of God! I invite you to allow the Lord to arouse you! To free you! To energize and motivate you! I invite you to open your eyes and ears along with your heart.

138 The Church doesn't need any more bureaucrats or functionaries! We need bold men and women to get up and do the work of the Reign of God—and true holiness leads to this kind of boldness. Like the saints, we will abandon "a dull and dreary mediocrity."

139 May the Holy Spirit now fill us with the courage to step out and get to work. May the Spirit move us out of an attitude of preserving the Church as a museum and make us into a throng of passionate disciples.

> **FOR GROUP PROCESS OR PERSONAL REFLECTION**
> *In your own words, define the sign of holiness that the*
> *Holy Father is teaching us here. How do you understand these*
> *elements of the spiritual life to fit into your call to holiness?*

IN COMMUNITY

140 Living alone and apart from others in an isolated world of our own makes it difficult for us to grow in holiness. We often give in to strong sexual desires or are lured into selfishness. We lose a sense of inner clarity.

141 We never journey to the heart of the Lord alone but always in community with others. We have publicly recognized small communities of Christians who, by living together, were filled with a level of courage and selflessness that they could not have achieved alone. As St. John of the Cross put it, "You are living with others in order to be fashioned and tried."

142 I invite you to join with others on your lifelong journey to holiness. Sharing the Eucharist together gives rise to communal intimacy and shared mystical experiences.

It draws us together and strengthens us, as it did for Saints Benedict and Scholastica or St. Augustine and his mother, St. Monica.

143 This shared, everyday, common life for most of us isn't filled with mystical moments. It's filled with the details of life. Joseph, Mary, and their son, Jesus, also lived an everyday life that was quite ordinary.

144 Jesus taught his followers to pay attention to the details around them. Whether it was running out of wine at a wedding, a single sheep missing from the flock, or the widow who offered just two small coins, it was in these details that their community was formed.

145 Holiness grows in the community as members care for each other and help each other see the Lord. By living together, we see that our efforts to care for and heal others lead us to profound divine joy.

146 I know this goes against the current social trend. Many people seek well-being alone and apart from others, but the path to holiness unites us with each other where we seek each other's well-being in the family of God.

FOR GROUP PROCESS OR PERSONAL REFLECTION

In your own words, define the sign of holiness that the Holy Father is teaching us here. How do you understand these elements of the spiritual life to fit into your call to holiness?

IN CONSTANT PRAYER

147 Finally, let us remember that holiness always leads to prayer. The prayer may not be lengthy, but it must be frequent and honest.

148 As St. John of the Cross reminds us, we should always try to be mindful of the presence of God and allow our hearts to turn to him freely and often throughout each day.

149 As it was for St. Teresa of Ávila, when we turn our hearts toward the Lord, we enter into personal and intimate conversation with Jesus, sharing concerns, hearing his voice correct and affirm us, and following his teachings. Such intimacy with Jesus isn't for a privileged few but for everyone. We can each learn to turn our heart to Christ in this way; it's an important element of holiness.

150 In the silence of our alone time with the Lord we discern our pathway to holiness, with the help of the Holy Spirit. If we don't enter into this quiet, prayerful time with Jesus, learning from him and listening to him, we become clanging gongs and noisy cymbals (1 Corinthians 13:1).

151 When we spend time in the presence of the Lord, even though we sin and are selfish, Jesus restores us to be fully human. Do you do this? Do you turn your heart toward him? Do you spend quiet moments alone with God? Do you love being in his presence, and do you let it inflame your heart with love? If you do not do this, holiness will be difficult to attain.

152 Never let prayer of this kind become an escape from the world. Don't reject the world but embrace it.

153 Prayer of this kind makes us mindful of all the good things that we have received. This prayer acknowledges our history, both the good and the sinful. When we remember how God has acted down through the years, it increases our gratitude and awareness of him.

154 Prayer of the heart is also the time when we ask God for the help we need, help for ourselves and the people of the world. We pray for others; we ask God to walk with them, heal them, and forgive them. Such prayer of intercession reflects the twofold commandment to love and trust in God while at the same time to love and care for our neighbor.

155 As Blessed Charles de Foucauld put it, once we have this intimate prayer time with the Lord, with Jesus, with Abba, and with the Spirit, we can do nothing other than live for God. As pilgrims on a journey to the heart of the Lord, we gaze on him, contemplate his love, and enjoy the silence.

156 Likewise we turn to Scripture with the same glad heart. Here we encounter the voice of the Master, a lamp for our steps, a light for our path. It transforms us.

157 And this leads us to the Eucharist, the highest form of prayer we know. Christ is uniquely and powerfully present to us in the Eucharist. We renew our covenant with him at the Eucharist, and we allow him to achieve the work of transforming us and the world.

FOR GROUP PROCESS OR PERSONAL REFLECTION

*In your own words, define the sign of holiness that the
Holy Father is teaching us here. How do you understand these
elements of the spiritual life to fit into your call to holiness?*

CHAPTER FIVE

Spiritual Combat, Vigilance, and Discernment

158 To live the Christian life, we must do battle with the prince of darkness and source of evil, the devil.

COMBAT AND VIGILANCE

159 The battle against evil is more than merely a struggle against a worldly mentality, and it's more than a battle against human weakness. "It's also a constant struggle against the devil." Jesus himself rejoiced when his disciples overcame the darkness.

More than a myth

160 Only when we understand life in all its supernatural elements can we come to understand the prince of darkness. This evil force is present among us. Indeed, in the story of the garden in Genesis, the evil one was present. Again, in the desert where Jesus faced temptations, he was present. When he taught us to pray, Jesus urged us to pray for deliverance from the evil one. This dark force is personal, and it is present.

161   This dark force poisons us like a snakebite with venom: hatred, envy, pride, despair. He can destroy our families, divide our communities, and bring all happiness to an end. He is indeed real and not a mere myth or figure of speech. We can never let down our guard.

Alert and trustful

162   The word of God instructs us about this evil force: "Quench all the flaming darts of the evil one," we are told in Ephesians 6:16. The path to holiness is a constant battle and those who fail to realize this will experience failure and mediocrity in the spiritual life. We do have tools to use in this fight: prayer, meditation, the Eucharist, reconciliation, works of charity, our community members, and the work of missionaries in our midst. These can help us identify the false promises of the prince of darkness.

163   The most powerful way to fight evil is to celebrate all that is good, all that is holy, and everything that leads to love. We can be confident in this: The Lord—who is the Light of the world—walks with us, and light is stronger than darkness.

Spiritual corruption

164   The Scriptures teach us to be vigilant in the spiritual life, to "keep our lamps lit" (Luke 12:35) and be ready. If we do this, we will know peace and joy on the journey. We must be ready, among other things, to admit our sinfulness; failing to do this results in a state of dull spiritual laziness. If we do not know that we have sinned, what need have we of being saved?

165   Those who are spiritually corrupt are also spiritually blind, which is harder to heal than those who know they are sinners. To the corrupt, everything seems normal. Even lies, slander, pride, and selfishness appear to be good—because the devil disguises himself as an angel. On the pathway to holiness, we must carefully guard our hearts and souls against this corruption; we must never think we are free of the snares of the evil one.

DISCERNMENT

166 The only way for us to know if something comes from God or the evil one is discernment. We must learn discernment and practice it, allowing prayer, reflection, reading, and the counsel of others to guide us in the discernment process.

167 In today's world we have many choices before us every single day. Some of them are mere distractions while others are full of immense possibility. How do we know the difference? Only through discernment. Without discernment, we will fall prey to every passing fancy.

168 We must always sort our options based on two possible scenarios. On the one hand, a new idea may be an illusion of good, a false promise offered by the prince of darkness. Following such ideas may corrupt the faith and lead to sin. On the other, new ideas may well be the work of the Spirit as it renews the Church in every age. Failing to adopt such new ideas may be resistance to this renewal, blocking the work of the Spirit. We have the freedom of Christ, who asks us to discern carefully. We must examine the urges within us: desires, fears, questions, and anxieties. And we must read the "signs of the times" to recognize where the pathway to freedom lies. "Test everything," we read in First Thessalonians 5:21; "hold fast to what is good."

169 We need discernment when facing major decisions, but we also need it in our daily lives to help us follow the Lord more closely. It helps us know God's timing on things; it helps us recognize our sins; and it helps us see good in others. I invite you to a daily "examination of conscience" so that you can learn to recognize specific ways in which the Lord is calling you.

A supernatural gift

170 Discernment of this kind doesn't ignore the work of psychology or sociology, but it does transcend it. Likewise, blindly following the rules of the Church is not sufficient. We can follow the rules without love, but it would do us no good. Discernment is a gift and a grace from God. It helps us glimpse the plan God has for each of us: What is the meaning of my life? To whom am I sent? How can I use my gifts to benefit the community? Discernment helps us answer these questions. It is not meant only for the well-educated; God reveals himself to everyone.

171 As I said above, a crucial element of discernment and holiness is the silence of prolonged prayer. We must turn our heart to Christ and open our ears, eyes, and heart to him. *Listen to him.* We will hear God speak. Within the fabric of our daily life, we find our orientation toward God because the Spirit empowers us.

Speak, Lord

172 Prayerful discernment only happens when we are ready to listen. It's possible for us to close ourselves off from God's voice, hearing only what we want him to say. We must also listen to those around us as well as to Scripture. In prayerful listening, we can set aside our usual way of seeing things and see them anew through God's eyes. God may call us out of our comfort into passionate and risky work. He may ask us to lead his people to freedom, to bear with suffering, or to go to the cross.

173 Listening, prayer, and discernment are rooted in obedience to both the gospel and the Magisterium of the Church. "It is not a matter of applying rules or repeating what was done in the past, since the same solutions are not valid in all circumstances and what was useful in one context may not prove so in another." The Spirit liberates us from rigidity and leads us to understand what the gospel demands of us in every new age.

The logic of gift and of the cross

174 It is essential that we learn to trust God's timetable in all discernment. We may feel hurried or impatient because God's time is not always ours. Discernment isn't about getting more out of life but about learning how we can "better accomplish the mission entrusted to us at baptism." We must be ready to sacrifice—to sacrifice everything if needed—for the sake of this mission. Giving up everything for Christ and our neighbor sounds illogical, but "our logic is the cross," as St. Bonaventure said.

175 In discernment we must allow God to touch every area of our lives, withholding nothing from him. Even in areas that we find uncomfortable, embarrassing, or difficult, God's hand will lead us to happiness. So, discernment isn't about analysis and introspection as much as about learning to leave ourselves behind as we approach the mystery of God.

FOR GROUP PROCESS OR PERSONAL REFLECTION

Describe how Christians discern God's call. What are the steps or elements of discernment? Why is it so important to a life of holiness?

Share about your experience of hearing the voice of God as it echoes in your depths. Read article 168 again and discuss how we "test" new ideas and grow in our understanding of what God is calling us to do and be.

---

* * *

176 I wish to crown these reflections by calling to mind Mary, the mother of Jesus. She lived the Beatitudes, rejoicing in God's presence and believing in the power of God. She is the saint among saints. If you want to learn the way of holiness, you only need to know Mary. When you pray, don't flood her with all your wordy concerns, but simply utter the simple phrase, "Hail, Mary." She is present.

177 I hope that these reflections will help the whole Church to grow in holiness. Come, Holy Spirit, fill the hearts of your faithful and kindle in us the fire of your love. "In this way, we will share the happiness that the world will not be able to take from us."

Also by
BILL HUEBSCH

 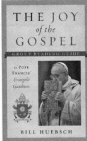  

THE JOY OF LOVE
A Group Reading Guide to Pope Francis' Amoris Laetitia

64 PAGES | **$4.95*** | **5½" X 8½"** | **9781627851985**

....

ON CARE FOR OUR COMMON HOME
A Group Reading Guide to Pope Francis' Laudato Si'

48 PAGES | **$3.50*** | **5½" X 8½"** | **9781627851220**

....

THE JOY OF THE GOSPEL
A Group Reading Guide to Pope Francis' Evangelii Gaudium

48 PAGES | **$3.50*** | **5½" X 8½"** | **9781627850193**

....

THE ART OF ACCOMPANIMENT
Four Essential Conversations on Becoming the Kind of Parish the Church Needs Today

48 PAGES | **$4.95*** | **5½" X 8½"** | **9781627852623**

*Sliding scale pricing available for bulk sales